Reflections for Women No. 2

by Ruth Johnson Jay

Back to the Bible
Lincoln, Nebraska 68501

80,000 printed to date—1981
(5-9889—80M—31)
ISBN 0-8474-1726-3

Cover photo by Bill Myers.

Printed in the United States of America

Contents

Subject **Page**

1. That Little Rascal 4
2. Oh to Be That Virtuous Woman 6
3. Those Ugly Stains 8
4. Patience! Patience! More Patience! 10
5. Getting Involved 12
6. Real Beauty 14
7. Those Special People 16
8. No Off-Limits Places 18
9. Can Any Good Come? 20
10. With Roses to Come 22
11. Immediately—If Not Sooner! 24
12. Always Needed 26
13. Those Communication Lines 28
14. Fear—Good or Bad? 30
15. Those Sleepless Hours 32
16. Anything Too Hard? 34
17. The Real Us 36
18. What Makes a Home? 38
19. Bring Them to Jesus 40
20. Prayer As Usual 42
21. Taking the Credit 44
22. Some Things Just Don't Matter 46
23. Which Prayers to Answer? 48
24. Ah! Those Memories 50
25. For Someone's Good 52
26. Those Childish Actions 54
27. His Flawless Ways 56
28. Inner or Outer Change? 58
29. That One Request 60
30. To Complain or to Thank? 62
31. It's Still There 64

1

That Little Rascal

BIBLE READING: James 3:7-18

That little rascal had done it again. My tongue had spouted off, producing sharp and unkind words.

Everything had gone wrong! (You know the feeling, don't you?) The car hadn't started, the vacuum-cleaner belt had broken, I had forgotten about the cake in the oven and, of course, it burned. By evening my nerves were beginning to fray like a piece of woven fabric. I should have stopped and calmly committed these problems to the Lord. Instead, I decided to work off my frustration.

I put up the ironing board, plugged the iron's cord into the socket and turned the dial to the wool setting. Pow! Something happened! The lights went out, the TV became quiet, the automatic washer came to an abrupt stop, and the iron refused to heat.

"What happened, Honey?" came a voice from the other room. "What happened?" I repeated, but my voice was harsh and angry.

What kind of question was that? Couldn't he see that I had blown a fuse? And didn't he remember how this whole day had gone? Now one more thing had added to my frustration. What happened? Everything happened!

Quietly my husband walked into the darkened room and put his arm tenderly around my waist. With the other hand, he reached for the flashlight. Then, wordlessly, he went to check out the fuse box.

On came the lights, the automatic washer and the television set. Even the iron began to crackle.

"What did you do?" I asked, for the moment not realizing that my question was just as silly as his had been. "You blow 'em, I fix 'em," he smiled.

Oh, that tongue; that rascal of a tongue had done it again. No! That wasn't the real problem. The tongue had only been the instrument for my heart. If, at that late hour of the evening, I had only sent up a distress signal to the Lord, things could have been so different. But I had tried to handle the problems in my own way. And I blew more than the fuse!

God reminds us that it is our privilege to come to Him at any hour—day or night. He does not ask us to work off our frustrations first and then ask for His grace. No, He has promised to supply all of our needs. All we have to do is come to Him.

ONE MORE THOUGHT: Why, oh why, do we think we should try everything in *our* power before we come to God for *His* power?

2

Oh to Be That Virtuous Woman

BIBLE READING: Proverbs 31:10-31

How do you compare with the virtuous woman in today's Bible reading? I can almost hear you argue that life for today's woman is much different than it was in those days. And you are right.

Among my problems today were a nonstick frying pan that stuck and a plate guaranteed not to crack that broke in half. And the glue I used to fix the plate (guaranteed never to give out) didn't even last through the day. How can I be a virtuous woman under those circumstances?

Even my shopping is much more difficult than it must have been for her. I go to the supermarket to buy food and come home with sacks full of paper towels, vacuum-cleaner bags and scouring powder! Today it's too easy to see something cute and very much in style and suddenly feel we need it. Supermarkets and department stores hire professionals to arrange their products just to lure women into impulse buying. The virtuous woman of Bible times didn't have these problems. She didn't even have television or soap operas to contend with.

As I read the verses again, I decide it's time to take inventory of what is really important in my life. The hours that come and so easily slip by, or are wasted, cannot be recalled. They come and they're gone.

Today's woman sometimes finds it difficult to set her priorities in order. It's easy to put things ahead of people and their needs. If God has entrusted to us a husband, a family and a home, then we must accept these as gifts from God, and they should be high on our priority list in time and importance.

The virtuous woman described in Proverbs 31 was concerned about the important things in life. Her husband trusted her judgment in buying wisely and caring properly for the needs of her family. Our virtuous woman was concerned for the poor, careful in her speech and quick to use her tongue to express kindness. She also had great fear, or reverence, for the Lord. (How do you fit the description so far?)

If we set our priorities straight and start the morning in a conversation with our Heavenly Father, asking Him for guidance through the day, help for the problems and love in every situation, sticky frying pans or broken dishes won't really change our disposition or our outlook on the day. They will just be insignificant incidents which pass by almost unnoticed.

Is this challenge too big to face? It shouldn't be for the woman committed to the Lord, the woman whose value is "far above rubies" (v. 10). No wonder her family loves her!

ONE MORE THOUGHT: Being a woman today may be a challenge, but being a virtuous woman as God has ordained may be an altogether different challenge.

3
Those Ugly Stains

BIBLE READING: II Samuel 11:1-17

What is the worst household job you have to tackle? Mine is oven cleaning. There is nothing that I can manage to put off any easier or any more often than cleaning a messy oven. And in spite of what all the TV commercials and magazine ads say, I have learned that none of the oven cleaners (not even the lemony one) makes the job a breeze. It's still hard work to try to get the oven to look like new. And the longer I put off the job, the harder it becomes. Those ugly, sticky spills almost seem to become a part of the oven after a time, and they are nearly impossible to remove.

I have learned, however, that the job is not nearly as depressing or difficult if I do it regularly. And an even better system is to clean it up after each use.

David had some ugly sins and stains to clean up too. His life was terribly marred with the sin of lust after Bathsheba. If David had immediately committed those lustful thoughts to the Lord and asked for forgiveness for them, both his life and the lives of those who came in contact with him could have been spared a great deal of grief. But instead, David chose to follow up on his desires. He called Bathsheba to come to him, and the stains were multiplied. But still David did not ask God for forgiveness.

Then Bathsheba told David she was pregnant. That would certainly have been the time for David to confess his sin and get things straightened out. But David thought otherwise. He plotted a cover-up. Calling for Bathsheba's husband, he made arrangements for him to come home from battle. That way the world would think that Uriah was the father of the baby.

But Uriah was a good soldier, and he refused to enjoy the pleasures of home and marriage while the others were fighting. Now what would David do? Confess? No, once again he plotted to clear himself. He ordered Bathsheba's husband to be put on the front lines where he was killed in battle.

What an awful progression of sin in David's life! How different everything would have been if only he had taken care of the "cleaning job" when it all began. But instead, he made matters worse by piling one unconfessed sin upon another.

Just as we should clean a soiled oven when the splatterings first appear, so we must confess our sin immediately and let God clean it up instead of our trying to cover it up.

ONE MORE THOUGHT: The world will tell us there are many methods for getting rid of the guilt of sin, but Jesus Christ is the only One who can do it.

4

Patience! Patience! More Patience!

BIBLE READING: I Kings 18:42-46

Do you recognize this scene?

The kitchen floor has just been scrubbed when out of nowhere comes that lovable little pup, the family pooch. He parades across the room as though he owns it, leaving his darling little pawprints all over the spotlessly clean floor. You scream at him, grab for the newspaper-switch and begin the wild chase all through the house. Suddenly you stop.

Say, now, aren't you the one who has been praying for more patience? Well, here's a touch of that tribulation the Bible promises to those who ask for patience (see Rom. 5:3). God, who knows all things, knew how serious you were when you petitioned Him for more patience, so He allowed a little four-legged tribulation to cross your kitchen path.

Patience is a strange thing. We want it, we need it, and we pray for it. But most of us are not overjoyed with the tribulation that helps to produce it in our lives.

Praying sincerely for specific needs often takes a great deal of patience. And it's so easy to give up when the answers do not come immediately. Some women have prayed for years for their drinking husbands, wayward children and unsaved relatives and have seen no obvious signs of an answer. But they prayed on and believed.

Elijah exercised patience and faith when he prayed for rain. Our Bible reading for today tells us that this man of God threw himself on the ground and humbly asked God to send rain. Then what? Did he forget about it until his prayer time the next day? No! Each time he prayed he sent his servant out to see if there was any sign of clouds in the sky.

Seven times Elijah petitioned God for rain. Six times the servant came back with the report, "There is nothing" (I Kings 18:43). But then came that seventh time. It wasn't much of a sign—Elijah's servant had seen a cloud, ever so small but, nevertheless, a cloud. The Bible tells us it was the size of a man's hand. Can you imagine how that servant had to squint to see a cloud that small in the faraway sky? Quickly he reported back to Elijah, and the man of prayer knew that God had sent the answer.

Are you praying for someone or something special? Keep on praying. It may be seven days or it could even be seven years or more before God sends that little sign. But send it He will. For as you pray and believe, God will honor your sincere and patient request.

ONE MORE THOUGHT: God does send signs from time to time to encourage us in our praying. Let's learn to watch for them.

5
Getting Involved

BIBLE READING: Esther 4:10-17

Jenny was a large, jovial woman who lived across the street from our home. Jenny had almost no education, but her heart was as big as the world. Everyone loved and respected this godly angel of mercy. She was always doing something for someone.

I can still remember the time she came to our home. Our mother was very ill; our father was out looking for a job. Jenny began giving orders to the children: "You do the dishes. You make the beds. You take the laundry downstairs." On and on she went until each of the six of us had specific jobs to do. Then she excused herself, assuring us that she would be back. But several hours passed before Jenny returned. When she did, there was a smile on her face and a prescription in her hand.

This wonderful Christian neighbor had spent the better part of the morning sitting in a doctor's office, waiting to get some medicine for her friend and neighbor. Jenny saw the need in our home, involved herself personally and did something about it. Because of her concern and involvement, our mother was up and around in a few short days.

In our Bible reading, we learned that Esther saw the need of her people. She knew that if someone did not do something, the Jews would most certainly be killed. Esther was a Jewess, and if she went to the king uninvited, revealed her nationality and made her petition, it could mean death for her too. Should she involve herself and take that chance? Or should she just step aside and let things happen as they would?

Esther saw the need. She cared enough about her people to get involved, and she acted on the problem. Through her intercession, her people were spared, and those who wanted to kill them were slain instead.

Dozens of needs come to our attention. People are hurting, crying for help. Some of our neighbors are without the spiritual guidance of a concerned Christian. Those of us who belong to the Lord can see those needs, and we are touched by what we see. But unless we get involved and do something about what we see, probably nothing will change.

Is there a spiritual need in your home, your church, your neighborhood? If so, are you willing to get involved and do something to reach those people for the Lord? You may feel you cannot leave your own neighborhood, but you can love. You may not be able to go to a foreign mission field, but you can give. And you may not be able to remedy every problem, but you can pray and try to help.

The world is full of needs, but the greatest needs are spiritual. Are you willing to get involved in some way to see that a needy person receives God's message of salvation?

ONE MORE THOUGHT: Care and concern are good, but they are not enough. Action and involvement are needed as well.

6

Real Beauty

BIBLE READING: Esther 2:12-18

"Get out of that bathroom! Go fix your face someplace else."

Does that have a familiar ring? Most women have probably heard similar words many times.

Down through the years women have had the reputation of spending untold hours fixing their hair, their faces, their eyes—themselves. We would never tolerate the accusation that we need more time and attention than men, but we do spend a great deal of time trying to cover up blemishes and improve our overall attractiveness.

Few performers go through life without a face-lifting and several dye jobs. But beauty treatments, cosmetics and perfumes are not new. In our Bible reading for today, we read that the young women who were to appear before King Ahasuerus spent a great deal of time preparing themselves for their introduction to him. It was not only a few hours, days or even weeks, but 12 full months! Any girl who was in line to meet the king had to be sure that she looked just right.

The cosmetic sales reports today show that women have not really changed down through the years. We still want to look young, beautiful and attractive—even when we aren't. Clothes, no matter what the price, play a big part in how we think, act, walk and look. And let's face facts: When people (including men) look at us as well-dressed, well-preserved and attractive women, we are flattered!

But a holy God is not really that concerned about the latest styles. He loves us as women, regardless of whether or not we have a clothing allowance, keep up with the latest styles, are beginning to fight wrinkles or have a sallow complexion. He created us, and He died for us. He is far more interested in how we look on the inside.

Cleanliness and care of our bodies are important, but inner purity must take priority in our lives. Some women spend hours "putting on their faces" but seem to find only minutes, and sometimes just a few seconds, to devote to that all-important inner preparation.

In Esther's day any woman who was to appear before the king had to go through a 12-month beauty treatment program. Oils, perfumes and cosmetics were used to improve her attractiveness. But all of these things could do nothing for the inner person. Esther's heart was in tune with her God, and it was this that brought out her true beauty.

Cosmetics and perfumes may or may not make us more interesting and attractive, but a heart filled with God's love will bring out the inner beauty He created us to have.

ONE MORE THOUGHT: The change brought on by a face-lifting may be striking, but the change brought about by a heart-lifting is far more impressive.

7

Those Special People

BIBLE READING: Genesis 22:3-13

Parents are special people! God has put into their hearts such a deep, indescribable love for their children that it is not always understood by those who have no children.

Abraham and Sarah were no exception. When God called on this family to sacrifice their only son on an altar, Abraham must have felt as though a knife were cutting him. But in spite of his deep and natural parental feelings, he was obedient to his Lord. Can't you almost feel the pain he must have experienced when Isaac asked him where the lamb for the sacrifice was? He must have been torn inside as he assured Isaac that God would provide a lamb. And yet Abraham continued. His love for God was greater than the tremendous love he had for his son.

How would you have reacted and responded if you had been Abraham? Wouldn't your hands have trembled as you began to tie the knots that would hold your child on the altar? It was, no doubt, difficult for Abraham, but it was not impossible because God was there to guide every step of the way.

A young high school student felt that God was leading her to attend Bible school rather than the state university where her folks had gone. As she explained the situation, her parents argued that she was "too brilliant" to waste her years in a Bible school. After some time they finally agreed to her choice of a school.

"We have just one request," said her mother. "Please don't come home and tell us that you want to go off to some far-flung mission field." The mother's words pierced the heart of the young teen, and the more she thought about them, the more they became a challenge. As a result, she committed her life in complete obedience to God to be used wherever He wanted.

The giving up of children is never easy. But this is what God required of Abraham. And it may be what He will require of you. Many parents stand before the pastor and the congregation, holding that precious little infant in their arms, and say, "He is yours, God; all yours." But what happens years later?

If God called upon you to give your child for His service and you knew there was a possibility of danger and death, could you do it? How deep is your love for God? Deep enough to trust Him with your children?

Parents are special people, and God has for them a special supply of grace.

ONE MORE THOUGHT: Some who have refused to give their children to God have later watched them fall into sin.

8

No Off-Limits Places

BIBLE READING: Acts 5:1-11

The "For Sale" sign was just being posted as we drove by the house. We learned that it was to be listed on the market the next day. The woman of the house was very cordial, allowing us to see the home before it was officially listed. Room after room, cupboards and closets were opened to us as the lady emphasized the good points to help promote a sale.

Then we came to another room. The door was closed. She put her hand on the knob. "I'm sorry," she admitted. "This room is off limits. It won't be ready to show until after tomorrow."

We were never told why that area was off limits, but we decided it must have been the room where everything was thrown whenever the family was in a hurry or when they wanted something totally hidden from view.

Many of us have off-limits places in our homes. Sometimes it's the attic, where treasured historical items have been tucked away until there is time to sort them out. Others use the basement as a convenient hideaway—anyplace where we can close the door and put out of mind what we do not want seen.

Some Christians carry this system into their spiritual walk as well. On Sunday mornings they make themselves look and act like the Christian they want people to think they are, forgetting or ignoring the fact that with God there are no off-limits areas. He knows and sees everything—even those areas that desperately need to be cleaned out. For some reason, we think those areas can be ignored if they are not seen.

Ananias and Sapphira had somewhat the same thought. They had agreed to lie. No one would know, or so they thought. But God knew, and so did the lying couple. Peter seemed to sense it too.

"Thou hast not lied unto men, but unto God," Peter said (Acts 5:4). Ananias immediately fell over—dead. Not long after he had been taken out and buried, his wife, who did not know of her husband's death, entered. Peter asked her, "Tell me whether ye sold the land for so much?" (v. 8). She answered, "Yea, for so much" (v. 8). Just as quickly, she, too, died and was buried beside her husband.

Verse 11 tells us that "great fear" came over the church. We, too, need to experience some fear when we consider holding out on some off-limits areas. Nothing can be hidden from God. There are no off-limits areas of our lives as far as He is concerned. He not only sees what our friends and neighbors see, but He also sees far more. His look penetrates the secret, hidden places of our lives. Nothing, absolutely nothing, is hidden from Him.

ONE MORE THOUGHT: Confession of sin can change "Off Limits" to "Open for Scrutiny."

9

Can Any Good Come?

BIBLE READING: Genesis 37:23-28

When things go wrong in spite of all our hard work and preparation, we often wonder, "Can anything good come from this?" Others have wondered this too. Joseph undoubtedly wondered how anything good could possibly come from his being thrown into a pit and then sold into slavery.

Our family was not wealthy. In fact, we were considered extremely poor, and many times we wondered if any good could come from such circumstances. Everyone in the family was somewhat musically inclined, but there was never enough money for voice or piano lessons. Our parents must have wondered if anything good would ever come of our musical abilities since they were not able to provide formal musical training. But each of us has had a musical ministry of one kind or another.

When situations around you become very trying, when bills pile up and money fails to come in, when your job suddenly comes to an abrupt end or when family problems become more than you can handle, perhaps you ask, "Can anything good come from this?" God's response is "Yes."

A young Mexican boy described how his family realized this. Because of his father's work, the family often had to move from one place to another. The children found it almost impossible to make any lasting friendships. When the boy was 16, there was another move, this time to a small house just outside the city. He became angry and in essence shouted, "Can any good come from this?"

But good did come from it. The house was owned by a Mexican Christian businessman. Each month when he came to collect the rent, he brought a small gift—a tract, a Bible, a gospel plaque. From these items, the children learned Bible verses and shared them with the other members of the family.

Before the year was over, the entire family had accepted Christ as Saviour. Had any good come from that move? Yes, God had not forgotten them.

Can any good come from the trials, the sickness, the marital difficulties or the problems with the children in your life?

Yes, good can come when we learn to commit *everything* to the Lord. Joseph learned this truth in Egypt. Though his brothers mistreated him, God allowed it because He had a greater plan for Joseph. Joseph was able to preserve his family and his nation during the years of famine in the land. As Joseph said, "Ye thought evil against me; but God meant it unto good . . . to save much people alive" (Gen. 50:20).

God has assured us, "All things work together for good to them that love God, to them who are the called according to his purpose" (Rom. 8:28).

ONE MORE THOUGHT: Good can come from anything when God is in charge.

10

With Roses to Come

BIBLE READING: John 11:5-15

From the first year of our marriage, my husband would have one dozen red roses delivered to our home each Valentine Day. For two or three days I would spend much of my time looking at them, smelling them and thoroughly enjoying the beautiful and meaningful tokens of love. But after only a few days my roses would be gone.

I loved the thought of getting red roses every February 14th, but one day I saw the price tag for the lovely flowers. My better judgment told me that this amount of money could be used more wisely if I would forego my February gift and we would use that money to buy rosebushes which could be planted in our own backyard.

The first Valentine Day after my noble suggestion, I felt a bit cheated. All day I watched as the delivery truck from the floral shop went up and down our street. Yes, it went right by our house. I knew there would be no roses delivered to our home that year. But that evening when I got my card, everything changed. With my husband's signature I also read: "With love; roses to come in June."

And come they did. Roses graced our home not only in June but also in July, in August and even into late September. Each day when the roses were brought into the house, my husband would say, "Happy Valentine Day."

The small sacrifice I made for one or two days in February was more than made up for by the enjoyment the roses brought in and around our home all summer and early fall.

Sometimes God chooses to withhold something from us because He knows the short-term answer is not nearly as good for us as the long-term blessings He wants to give later. We may feel a bit cheated at the time because our prayers were not answered as we thought they should have been. But we can have confidence that God's ways are perfect and cannot be improved upon.

Mary and Martha must have felt a little cheated too. They had sent word to Jesus, telling Him that their brother was very sick. But Jesus did not arrive when they expected Him. Instead, He deliberately waited because He knew what the end results would be. Our Lord wanted to use this sickness to show His miracle-working power. Mary and Martha must have chided themselves later for ever questioning their Master. They had hoped He would come immediately and make their brother well. But God knew that bringing a dead man back to life would be a stronger witness of His power to the many who stood by and watched.

Sometimes we forget that God's ways are far superior to our ways. But the truth remains that His long-term blessings often far outweigh our short-term wishes. Let's allow Him to work as He wants to work in our lives.

ONE MORE THOUGHT: Allowing God to answer our prayer in His own way and in His own time is well worth the waiting we may have to do.

11

Immediately—If Not Sooner!

BIBLE READING: I John 1:5—2:2

What would this old world be like if all of us would apologize immediately after doing something wrong? Imagine getting things straightened out as soon as we sinned! There would be fewer hard feelings. Seldom would there be a reason to hold a grudge (not that there is now). The air would be cleared quickly, and better communication and understanding would be the result. Does that sound like a dream world?

I grew up in a home where the dishwashing chores were almost always handled this way. Dirty dishes weren't allowed to be left uncared for. Immediately after dinner, the person whose turn it was to wash the dishes left the table and, without a detour to some other part of the house, headed right for the kitchen sink. Each of us not only took our turn at washing and drying the dishes, but we also tried to convince our mother that a family the size of ours should seriously consider using paper plates. But like the dirty dishwater, our suggestion went down the drain, and we were stuck with the job!

However, our mother had what we considered a good system. I liked it as a child and have often found myself following it as an adult. While the gravy was simmering in the roaster or the food was being placed on the table, Mom was standing over the kitchen sink scrubbing out the pots and pans. She knew that if the messy pans were left until the meal was over, they would take much more scrubbing to get clean. And that, she knew, would give us an opportunity to try to convince her that pots and pans should be soaked overnight!

Our Bible reading for today seems to indicate that Mom's system really works when used in connection with our Christian walk. When we sin—and we do so often—we should go directly (without detours or excuses) to our Heavenly Father and confess that sin. God, who is "faithful and just" (I John 1:9), will then forgive us. Isn't that wonderful? The One who knows our weaknesses is also willing to forgive us when we come to Him.

And wouldn't it be wonderful if all Christians would immediately confess their sins and apologize to one another instead of putting it off? Those old sins that we allow to build and fester until they become so hard to confess and put aside could be immediately forgiven and forgotten.

Pots and pans with sticky or dried-on food were seldom found in the old kitchen sink in our home, but only because mother took care of the clean-up job immediately.

What a lesson for all Christians!

ONE MORE THOUGHT: The longer we allow our sins to "set," the harder God will have to "scrub" us in the clean-up process.

12
Always Needed

BIBLE READING: II Timothy 1:1-9

If your home has been blessed with children, you know how much each child depends on his mother's being around when he needs her. From the day of birth, the care and love of Mother is of utmost importance in the life of that infant. As he crawls, raises himself and takes that first step, he has no fears, for Mother is there, and she will catch him if he should lose his balance and fall.

The healthy child begins to run and play, and that most certainly means some falls and bruises. But once again, Mother is there to kiss those hurts and to care for the bruised elbows and knees.

And then come the teen years, the time when Mother often feels that her child has become so independent that he no longer seems to know she is around. She is crushed as she feels she has been brushed out of his life. And then something happens, and suddenly he lets her know how vital she really is.

High school and college days quickly pass, and one day her child is married. Certainly she won't be needed now. He has a wife, and all his thoughts are on her. Then the telephone rings, and there is his voice. Something serious must have happened for him to call. But in answer to her question he says, "No, Mom. I just felt like I wanted to talk with you." Her day is made. He still needs her love, her fellowship and her prayers.

Did you ever wonder how God must feel as He sees His children go through life? In those early days, shortly after conversion, there seems to be a constant need to call on the

Saviour. The new Christian needs wisdom and help to walk and grace to rise again when he falls.

But how many times the communion and communication end there. As the Christian grows and becomes more mature, he also seems to feel more independent. At times God is left out of the picture. And then suddenly something happens, and God gets that long-awaited "call." Sometimes it is because of sickness, sometimes there is a need for guidance. Sometimes it's because of the death of a dear one. But how pleased God must be when one of His children "calls" just to talk—no big crisis, just a lonely feeling and a need for fellowship.

God loved us enough to give us spiritual birth. He cared for us and led us through those early, unstable years of our faith. But how much time have we given Him "just to keep in touch"? When we spend time with Him, the blessing is ours.

ONE MORE THOUGHT: God is there to hear us when we have a special need. But how pleased He must be when we come to Him just because we want to talk.

13

Those Communication Lines

BIBLE READING: Psalm 63:1-6

Sometimes I am really bothered by that telephone company nuisance we have in our house. More often than not, it rings when I'm cleaning the garage, so I have to dash in and rinse off my hands before I dare touch the receiver. Or it will ring when my hair is foaming with shampoo. By the time I reach the phone, the party has given up, and all I get in response to my "hello" is a monotonous dial tone. When I do get to it in time, the doorbell is sure to ring, or the meter man will show up. And during long-distance calls, someone is sure to pull into the driveway and knock at the back door, demanding my immediate attention. There are times when I consider the telephone an unnecessary piece of equipment.

And then something happens. Someone gets sick, and we need a doctor. Or there is an accident, and an ambulance must be called. Or my husband has some good news to share with me, and he takes time out of his busy day to call. Yes, at times such as that I am so thankful for the telephone.

I am also glad we have a phone when someone with a deep need calls to share a burden. Sometimes tears are shed on both ends of the line; sometimes one is stronger than the other. But either way, how nice to hear the voice of someone who considers you a friend and who will listen, understand and perhaps even help.

At such a time my thoughts go not to the telephone company but to my private "line" to God. There is no time of the day or night that He is not waiting to hear from me. His line is available to me at all times, and He knows ever so well when I find it hard to talk—even to Him. He doesn't care if I just kneel there and shed a few tears of sorrow or repentance before I can say a word. He loves me for it.

At those times I realize how important it is to keep the lines clear and ready for those emergency "calls." But the communication system between the Saviour and His children is useful for far more than just emergency calls. God wants me to call and tell Him I love Him. He waits for me to share some wonderful, happy experiences with Him. And He doesn't care how many times I may be interrupted while I'm talking to Him. He's always there when I return.

This is when I realize how important He is to me and how I must never allow anything to cut the lines from here to heaven.

ONE MORE THOUGHT: Prayer is the telephone system between my heart and God. The Bible is His way of communicating with me. I need both.

14

Fear—Good or Bad?

BIBLE READING: Psalm 112

Fear is a strange thing, and it produces different reactions in different people. Hardly a child is not afraid when he hears, "Just wait until your father comes home!" This statement has caused some to live in constant fear until Father has administered the punishment. Others figure out how to get away with their "crime" because Father is not a threat.

In some Christian families, children learn a form of hypocritical fear right at home. They see Father driving down the highway in excess of the posted speed limit—until he hears on the CB radio that there are police in the area. Then he slows down because he is afraid of being stopped. Children also hear Mother's complaints that she is taking her turn in the church nursery or helping with the cleaning jobs only because she is afraid she will be criticized if she does not.

For some, the fear of being a failure is so strong that they avoid doing the things they enjoy. Some individuals fear being alone, being criticized or appearing ignorant about certain subjects.

Fear is said to have been responsible for keeping some teens from stealing, taking drugs or otherwise following in the careless footsteps of their peers. Some Christians confess that the only reason they continued to attend church during their difficult teenage years was the fear of explaining their absence to their parents. While such fear may produce positive results in some cases, attitudes toward church attendance and good, moral living demands a much stronger motive than fear alone. A person needs to have a healthy respect for doing that which is right.

The Bible speaks about fear in a different way. It tells us to fear the Lord—to have a reverential respect or awe of Him. This kind of fear is the beginning of wisdom, said the psalmist (Ps. 111:10).

The Lord referred to Job as a man "that feareth God" (Job 1:8). Job was not afraid of God; rather, he had a healthy love for God, demonstrated in his continuing obedience to Him.

In the New Testament we read that Cornelius, a centurion, was a just man and "one that feared God" (Acts 10:2). He loved and respected the Lord.

As we read these verses, we need to ask ourselves whether we fear God because we are not living as we should and are afraid of punishment or whether we have genuine love and reverence for the Lord.

ONE MORE THOUGHT: We do not need to be afraid if we fear (reverence) the Lord.

15

Those Sleepless Hours

BIBLE READING: Psalm 121

The digital clock seemed like such a good idea when we first bought it. The fact that it had a lighted dial on it appealed to me. Imagine waking up at any hour of the night and being able to see the exact time.

But on those nights when sleep doesn't come too easily, a digital clock can be a real nuisance. You look at it and see that it is 1:13 a.m. Then what you think is an hour later turns out to be 1:17 a.m. The longer you lie there, the more convinced you become that you have been awake for hours. But another look at the digital clock reveals that it is now exactly 1:27 a.m. For some reason, looking at that clock makes a sleepless night seem even longer than it actually is.

The night hours seem to go by more slowly than the daytime hours. You try every method you know for getting to sleep, and none of them work. You count more sheep than Australia can produce in a year. You pray for every missionary you know and silently recite dozens of Scripture verses—all the time wishing you had memorized many more. And still sleep does not come.

Someone has suggested thinking about the many Bible references that have to do with activities in the night hours as a cure for insomnia. You can remind yourself that when God created the world, there was nothing but darkness. Then He said, "Let there be light: and there was light" (Gen. 1:3). A New Testament passage reminds you that Jesus, who is the Light of the World, takes away the darkness of life (John 8:12).

Thank Him for forgiving your sins, and remember that He also said, "Ye are the light of the world" (Matt. 5:14). Pray for those who are still living in spiritual darkness.

By now you are either asleep, or else you are having such a wonderful time with the Lord that you don't want to go to sleep. If you're still awake, you can think about passages that tell how Job tossed through the night hours (Job 7:4) and how Paul and Silas sang when they could not sleep in prison (Acts 16:25). (If you try this method, do it silently!) Finally, remind yourself that God's love and grace are just as sweet during the sleepless night hours as they are during the day. God cares for us—day or night. When the burdens of the family or the problems of the day rob you of the relaxing sleep you need, remember that these hours can be very important to your spiritual life if they are committed to God.

It is very possible that these many suggestions for finding sleep may not make you sleepy at all, but just think of the marvelous time you will be having with your Lord. And isn't that worth it all?

ONE MORE THOUGHT: God, who cares for His children 24 hours a day, can sometimes get our attention only during those sleepless night hours.

16
Anything Too Hard?

BIBLE READING: Genesis 18:9-14

Mary Slessor had known since she was a young girl that someday she would be a missionary to Africa. She had read stories about David Livingstone and had listened as missionaries talked about their work in that land.

Because Mary's father used most of the family income for alcohol, the girl's education had been neglected. But Mary determined to prepare herself for that "someday" mission. She knew that God would find a way for her to reach the continent of Africa. It looked impossible at times, but God did not forget her.

Her trust in God brought her through the many months of preparation and eventually got her to the field of service to which God had called her. She knew the answer to that question which God had asked Sarah: "No, nothing is too hard for the Lord."

The great scientist, George Washington Carver, was the child of a slave girl. He was sold to a family who cared for him through many days of sickness. Because he was a sickly black boy living with a white family, many people shunned him. At school the other children made fun of him, but God did not desert George Washington Carver. Instead, He led him to do great things.

While other scientists looked only into a microscope for answers, George also looked up to his God. He knew the strength of God's Word: "Is any thing too hard for the Lord?" (Gen. 18:14).

Is there a problem in your household, one that seems to grow bigger and bigger every passing day? A wayward son, a sick husband, a lack of money or some other seemingly impossible problem? God asks, "Is any thing too hard for the Lord?" (v. 14).

Is not God able to redirect the life of that wayward child? Doesn't He know when the family needs money or that a loved one is sick? Of course He knows, and He cares. And when He whispers, "Is any thing too hard for the Lord?" He waits for the reply, "No, Lord. Nothing."

Sarah's situation was humanly impossible to understand. At the age of 90, with her husband 100 years old, how could they have children? "Impossible," says a doubting world. But God asked, "Is any thing too hard for the Lord?" (v. 14).

ONE MORE THOUGHT: If nothing is too hard for the Lord and if we, His children, are controlled by Him, then nothing is too hard to believe. So trust Him.

17
The Real Us

BIBLE READING: Luke 10:38-42

What is your reaction when someone pulls out the old family photo album and begins to turn the pages of history—your history? Does something happen inside of you when the room fills with uncontrollable laughter and a young voice squeals, "You didn't really look like this, did you?" It's not always complimentary to hear, "Oh, wow! Did you really look like this?" After such a question, you're not sure whether you should be pleased that you're considered a "one-time" beauty or whether you should be upset because someone noticed how much your appearance has changed! A mad dash to the mirror confirms the fact that there most certainly has been a drastic, not-necessarily-for-the-better change. The mirror shows the real person.

Or does it? Are you really the person in the photo album or the image in the mirror? Tall or short, fat or thin, young or old—is that the real person, the real you?

No, God doesn't see us that way. When He looks at us, His eye penetrates deeper than either the mirror or the camera. God looks beyond the facial expressions and the outward actions; He looks down into the heart. It doesn't matter to Him if the skin is wrinkled or smooth, the hair blond or gray. God sees us as we are. He sees qualities that go far deeper than the smoothness or color of skin. Yes, He sees us exactly as we are.

And what are we? Women overly concerned about getting the laundry done or the house cleaned? Does God see us as frustrated individuals, puttering and sputtering as we prepare the meals and clean up for the family?

Or does He see women with hearts of love and concern, busy about our various duties but accepting these chores as part of the ministry that God has entrusted to our care?

Yes, we are more than what can be seen in a photo or a mirror, much more. We are His workmanship, created in His likeness.

But because a sinful world cannot see us as God sees us, it is of utmost importance that our outward appearance reflect our relationship to Christ.

ONE MORE THOUGHT: It's easy enough to pretend to be something we are not. But only with God's help can we actually be what He expects us to be.

18

What Makes a Home?

BIBLE READING: Esther 1:1-8

Those soap-opera living rooms! Have you seen them and maybe even envied the people who "live" in them? Imagine how wonderful it would be to have a velvet couch with drapes to match and beautiful, but breakable, crystal on every end table, in spite of the fact that there are children in the family! And tell me, have you ever seen the daily newspaper strewn across a soap-opera floor? And how is it that the children's toys, which never seem to be picked up at your house, are stacked away in an orderly toy box in the corner of that perfect room?

And Mother! She walks around in a long, flowing caftan with full sleeves, never looking unkempt. She never seems to have dishes to do, a room to clean or a bathroom to scrub! Oh boy, what a life!

King Ahasuerus's garden was similar to these "prop" living rooms we see on the tube. The drapes were made of white and blue linen (Esther 1:6). And the drape cords were fastened to silver rings (v. 6). And did you notice the description of the couch? Silver and gold, placed on a mosaic pavement of marble (v. 6).

Just like your house. Right? Hardly!

But in spite of these costly furnishings, neither King Ahasuerus nor the soap-opera characters seem to display true happiness. There is always some deep problem in the TV story, and in spite of the fact that the king threw a big party for all the leaders in his kingdom, he wasn't too satisfied with life either.

You see, happiness does not depend on drapes or couches. It is not dependent on a nice wardrobe or even on model children. True happiness has little to do with household furnishings, but everything to do with the attitude and mood of the woman of the house. Her cheerful outlook on life is of vital importance to the happiness of her family. A complaining woman is no joy to come home to for either her husband or her children. But if the woman expresses contentment and happiness, the family will most likely reflect the same outlook and attitude.

Society tries to dictate our roles, endeavoring to make us discontent with our home life, with our children and with our family responsibilities. But as Christian women, we must recognize our God-given call and position and accept it in a loving way.

Let's not let a sinful world dictate either our wants or our responsibilities. Let's be what God wants us to be at home, at work or wherever we are. A godly woman is one of His creations, content and willing to be and to do what He wants of her.

ONE MORE THOUGHT: Furniture cannot make a home, but women often do.

19

Bring Them to Jesus

BIBLE READING: John 1:29-42

She was just a teenager, but her face showed signs of distress, hatred and unhappiness. Her short-term marriage was over, and she had turned again to drinking and drugs. But they hadn't helped. Miserable as she was, she had attempted suicide, but she hadn't even been successful at that.

What she needed was the Lord. Why hadn't someone shown her the way to salvation? How different her life could have been if someone had just brought her to the Lord Jesus.

Down through the centuries lives have been changed because someone brought someone else to Jesus. When Andrew met the Lord, he went out to find his brother. And the Bible tells us that Andrew "brought him to Jesus" (John 1:42).

Someone brought Dwight L. Moody to Jesus, and as a result, thousands came to Christ through his evangelistic ministry. Someone brought David Livingstone to Jesus, and when he later shared the message of salvation with Africans, many believed and were saved. Someone brought J. Hudson Taylor to Jesus, and China was touched with the gospel.

This pattern still works today. Someone brought your pastor to Jesus, and today his preaching is benefiting those in his congregation. Someone brought my father and mother to Jesus. Through their influence, six children came to know Christ as Saviour and Lord.

Is there someone you know who needs to be brought to Jesus? Who is it? They may have insurmountable problems that look as though they can never be solved. But as you introduce them to Jesus and as they surrender themselves to Christ, He can change their lives and solve their problems as well.

What would have happened if Andrew had met Jesus and had rejoiced in the fact that he had seen the Messiah but had never shared that joy with Peter? Peter would not have preached on the Day of Pentecost. He would not have been included among the three beloved disciples who walked close to our Lord. We would not have the benefit of Peter's influence in our lives. We would not have known how he suffered when he followed Christ afar off (Luke 22:54), how he wept when he denied his Lord (v. 62) or how he cautioned believers to "grow in grace, and in the knowledge of our Lord and Saviour Jesus Christ" (II Pet. 3:18).

Aren't you glad that Andrew "brought [Peter] to Jesus" (John 1:42)? Isn't there someone whom you should bring to Him?

ONE MORE THOUGHT: Will someone one day thank God because somebody brought you to the Lord, and you, in turn, brought them?

20
Prayer As Usual

BIBLE READING: Daniel 6:10-16

A young family was sitting in a busy restaurant waiting to be served when the youngest member of the group called out, "Dad, aren't we going to pray?" A bit embarrassed, the parents quickly explained that when they were in a public eating place, they didn't usually pray. "Why?" insisted the child. "Don't we tell God thanks for the food we get here?"

Many families have wondered what to do about prayer in public. Some people find it as easy to do there as they do at home, while others bow their heads, rub their forehead or eyes and silently breathe "a quickie."

It is often a little harder to bow for prayer when we are in public than when we are at home. This is especially true when we are sitting there all by ourselves.

Daniel faced a somewhat similar problem, but he had no trouble deciding what he should do. He knew that a petition had been made and signed by a king. No one was to make any prayers to "God or man for thirty days" unless it was to King Darius (Dan. 6:7). How easy it would have been for Daniel to go along with the decree, telling himself that there was nothing he could do about it. The law was the law, and it had to be obeyed, or he would suffer the consequences—being thrown into the den of lions.

But Daniel had made a habit of opening his windows, kneeling down and praying and giving thanks to God three times a day. He did not do this to show off his spirituality; it was something he had always done and firmly believed in. So in spite of the law, Daniel continued his prayer times "as he did aforetime" (v. 10).

The men who had instigated the law had tried earlier to find something against Daniel, and they had been unsuccessful. But knowing of Daniel's custom to pray, they went to his home to see whether or not he would obey the new law.

And what did Daniel do? Exactly as he had done before the new law took effect. The presidents and princes watched; there he was, opening the window and praying to his God. We are familiar with the outcome. Daniel was caught, the matter was reported to the king, and Daniel was thrown into the den of lions. Prayer was so meaningful to this Hebrew that he was willing to risk death to continue his practice.

What have we had to suffer during our prayer time? A little embarrassment perhaps, but that is all.

Are we willing to let someone laugh or criticize us in order to teach our families to continue to do as we have done "aforetime"?

ONE MORE THOUGHT: How much does prayer mean to us if we can so easily set it aside?

21

Taking the Credit

BIBLE READING: John 1:19-28

A newspaper reporter was standing backstage waiting to interview one of the outstanding pianists of the concert stage. Near him stood an elderly woman.

"Are you a family member?" he asked, hoping to talk to someone who knew the pianist well.

She shook her head. "No," she confessed. "But neither you nor that pianist would be here today if it hadn't been for me."

Her statement created keen interest, and the reporter asked the woman to explain her statement. She went on to say that she had been the pianist's first piano teacher. The reporter recorded her comments and continued the interview.

The woman had not lied in her statement. It was true that she had been his first piano teacher. But what she failed to tell the reporter was that the now-great pianist had quit after his fourth lesson.

Most of us like to take credit for the things we do and, at times, even for the things we don't actually do. Oh, we wouldn't lie, but we will certainly make every effort to get any credit that might possibly come our way. We enjoy having people think more highly of us than they ought to think.

John the Baptist was not like that. He had every opportunity to boast about his ministry when the Jews asked him who he was. He could have truthfully reported on the large crowds who came to be baptized by him. Or he could have emphasized the fact that he had been chosen of God to be the forerunner of Christ. But John did not do that. Instead, he said simply, "I am not" (John 1:20). John the Baptist made sure that these people understood that he was not the Messiah, not the Lamb of God who could take away the sins of the world. Question after question was answered, "I am not." Then simply and humbly he explained that he was merely a voice for the One who was to come (see v. 23).

In this day and age when the media publicize stories of what people have done, it's hard not to boast about the things that we have actually accomplished. But God, who knows our hearts, also knows what our part has been in any service. For every person in the limelight, several people have undoubtedly been in the background to aid in that person's success.

John confessed that he was not the important one but merely a forerunner sent to prepare the path of the Messiah.

This should be our attitude too—humble, sincere, not seeking glory for ourselves even when God allows us to be successful in what we do.

ONE MORE THOUGHT: God does not call many of us to be outstanding leaders, but He has called all of us to be faithful servants.

22

Some Things Just Don't Matter

BIBLE READING: Genesis 19:22-26

When a newspaper advice columnist received a second letter from a lady, she read it carefully and decided to feature it in her next column. In her first letter the lady had complained bitterly about her husband's snoring. "I can't stand it another day," she had written. Her second letter stated simply, "It is no longer a problem; I wish it were. My husband died of a sudden heart attack. I'd give anything if the bedroom were not so quiet."

Sometimes women find it difficult to balance important things against those that are less important. We tend to let little things irritate us; we have been known to make them almost a matter of life or death.

For example, suppose you have just spent the better part of an hour scrubbing and scouring the bathroom. You step back and look at your labor of love and admire the new shine on the tub, the sparkle of the faucets and the fact that there are no water spots on the mirror.

You are just admiring your work of art when two little soiled hands appear. The faucet is turned on (full force, of course), splashing water and dirt from one end of the room to the other. You glance quickly at the mirror and notice that water is running down it like a stream.

The soap dish takes on a grimy look too. And what dirt is not left on the bar of soap suddenly appears on the clean white towel behind you.

As you scan your once beautifully clean room and remember

all the time you spent scrubbing it, you wonder how two small hands could do so much damage in such a short time.

You make a big scene about it and then slip quietly into another room to think things over. You ask yourself what you would do if God took your complaints seriously and decided to take those little hands away, since they cause you so many insurmountable problems. Just think, the mirror would never show water spots. The soap dish would be clean, and there would be no more dirty fingerprints on the towel. That's when you decide that some things really don't matter.

Lot's wife had trouble with her priorities too. When God promised to help Lot and his wife escape from the wicked city, "Mrs. Lot" decided she just had to have one more look at the old hometown. The result? She died.

Some things *are* important, such as the spiritual needs of our families. Other things really don't matter. We need to learn how to tell the difference. This can be done only as we realize the importance of spending time with our Lord, asking Him for wisdom in the things that matter.

ONE MORE THOUGHT: Paying less attention to things that don't matter may give us more time for the things that do matter.

23

Which Prayers to Answer?

BIBLE READING: Romans 8:25-32

It was Christmas, and we were finally going to have a couple of days of vacation. Because we lived so far away from the other members of our family, we seldom saw them. So the anticipation of the short Christmas visit grew with every hour.

It had started to snow earlier in the day. A beautiful, soft, white blanket of flakes covered the ground, adding to the beauty of the holiday season. But soon it was no longer just a lovely snow. Reports indicated accumulations of five inches and then seven inches. Finally, nearly a foot of the white stuff was predicted.

Thirty minutes before we were to leave, we listened to the radio for a last-minute report. "Hazardous driving," said the announcer. "The highway department does not recommend travel."

It wasn't fair! The one time when we had a chance to get away, this awful weather was obviously going to keep us from it.

A farmer's wife walked into our shop, stomping the snow off her feet. "Merry Christmas!" she shouted happily. "And wasn't it good of God to send this wonderful snow?"

Before I could grumble to her about how God's snow had just spoiled our entire weekend, she went on. "We lost almost everything this past year," she said softly. "It was so dry that we knew another year without moisture would force us to leave the farm. This snow is an answer to prayer."

I glanced over toward my husband and then quickly turned

away. How did God know which prayer to answer? We had prayed for good weather for traveling, but these farm people had prayed for moisture for their crops—food for themselves as well as a hungry world.

In spite of our disappointment, we sensed God's leading as the snow continued to come down steadily. I knew that I would thank the Lord next summer as we enjoyed the produce from the fields. And if I could thank Him then, why not now?

I thought again about the Christmas season. The true meaning of the season was far more than a quick trip to see the relatives, as nice as that might be. It was Christ's coming to this world to live and to die for sinful people. It was love—God's love for a spiritually hungry world.

As the last customer of the day left our store, my disappointment had subsided measurably. After all, there was no reason we could not worship the Saviour here at home as well as 200 miles away.

ONE MORE THOUGHT: God hears many and varied requests. And yet He never makes a mistake in answering any of them. His answer may not always be our way, but His perfect way is best.

24
Ah! Those Memories

BIBLE READING: II Timothy 1:1-8

We came from all parts of the country—my brothers and sisters and I. And even though we hadn't all been together for more than ten years, it took only a few minutes for us to get into the "Do you remember when?" routine. Memories—some were pleasant, some were sad.

A young mother was sharing some of her Christmas memories with a friend. "All I can remember is my father's coming home drunk and falling into the Christmas tree," she admitted. Her thoughts brought back unpleasant memories.

What are your memories of home? Are they pleasant or unhappy? Or more important, what will your children's memories of home be? Will they recall inconsistencies, bad tempers and unkind words? Or will they remember a mother who prayed and a father who cared? Will they think back on some precious times in God's Word?

When Paul wrote to Timothy, he reminded his young friend of the spiritual inheritance that was his because of a godly mother and grandmother. When Timothy looked back, he could remember a home where God had been honored, and undoubtedly his memories of the past were mostly happy ones.

Paul also reminded his spiritual son of some other "remembrances." Timothy was told to keep in mind (remember) the gift that God had given him (see II Tim. 1:6). Paul did not want young Timothy to forget the fact that his gift was from God.

How easy it is to take our gifts for granted and to forget that

God is the source of all our talents and gifts. James 1:17 reminds us, "Every good gift and every perfect gift is from above."

God has showered many wonderful blessings on us. But how often have we taken time to think about them and to thank Him for each one? One important blessing that we often forget is a godly mother. Timothy had that.

If you come from a Christian home, you have many memories for which to be thankful. I remember a father who insisted on taking all of us to church twice on Sunday and a mother who managed to get each of her six children ready in time for those all-important Sunday activities. What a blessing! What a memory!

Whether your childhood home was godly or ungodly, as a believer you now have the solemn responsibility to see that your family will be able to look back to memories that are Christ-honoring and God-fearing. Are you fulfilling that responsibility?

ONE MORE THOUGHT: You are building memories each day. How will your family react when they "remember when"?

25

For Someone's Good

BIBLE READING: Psalm 48:1-13

Sometimes we read factual Bible stories as though they were events from some storybook. We talk about the experiences of Daniel in the den of lions and Jonah in the inner being of the huge fish as though they were simply some thrilling or frightening fiction stories. But they were real, and I for one would not care to be found in either of those places!

Jonah went through his trying experiences because of sin in his life (see Jon. 1). He was trying to run away from God's call. He agreed to serve God all right, but it was to be in his way and in his choice of location. Since Jonah refused to listen to God and follow His leading, it was necessary for the Lord to open the mouth of the huge fish and put His servant through an unusual and uncomfortable experience.

Daniel, on the other hand, was not disobedient to the Lord. He was one of the few men of his day who was living close to his God. In spite of the decree that men were not to pray, Daniel knelt three times each day as he had always done (see Dan. 6). When he was thrown into the den of lions, God closed the mouths of the lions so they would not harm His faithful servant. And because God shut the mouths of the lions, Daniel was unharmed, even though he spent an entire night in a den of vicious animals.

Sometimes Christians say they are suffering for Christ's sake or going through deep waters of spiritual suffering when, in reality, they are going through these things because of their own foolishness. Some of these experiences may even be chastening from the Lord because of disobedience or unbelief.

God has promised to take care of us through every situation. He did not promise to keep us from going through some trying times, but He has promised to go with us. There are times when He chooses not to close the "mouths" of the "animals" so that we will more readily learn some important lesson.

These two well-known stories are in God's Word for our good. As we read them we should learn the lesson that God wants us to learn. Jonah was gulped down by the large fish in order to show him what God wanted of him. Daniel had to go through his frightening experience to show the king what power God had.

Sometimes we are called upon to go through experiences for our own good, sometimes for the good of others. If God should call on us for this task, will we be as faithful as Daniel?

ONE MORE THOUGHT: No experiences "just happen" to the Christian. Everything is planned and worked out by God for someone's good.

26

Those Childish Actions

BIBLE READING: Genesis 3:8-19

My parents came to the United States from Sweden, so they found it easier to express themselves in their mother tongue. We had heard that language in our home all our lives, so there was little that we did not understand.

But if for some reason we did not particularly want to do whatever it was our parents were asking at the time, we would "play ignorant" and pretend not to be able to understand their instructions. It was a silly, childish act on our part, and I doubt very much that we ever fooled our folks, but as children we thought we did.

Often God, our Heavenly Father, uses His Word to talk to us. At times we decide that we want to ignore what is stated so clearly, so we pretend not to understand what the passage is saying. Young people particularly use this method. They argue that the Bible is hard to understand, so they can't be expected to read it. They think they are fooling both their parents and God. But this is a childish trick, and the only one being fooled is the young person himself.

And age does not always determine who plays this game. Mothers and fathers, husbands and wives—many adults—use it when they want to take part in something they know is not godly. But God knows the heart. He knows whether you are living carelessly and have a desire for worldliness or whether you have genuinely misunderstood what He has said in His Word.

The Bible is our guidebook. It contains a clear message for

everyone—milk for the new Christian and meat for the maturing saint. We have no excuse for not obeying its counsel because when there is a genuine lack of understanding, the Holy Spirit is there to help us and to open our eyes to the truths that will lead us where we should go.

After Adam and Eve had sinned, they decided they would play a little game with God. Like small children they ran and hid, thinking that perhaps the great Creator would not know where they were hiding. What a childish notion! Had not God created the world and everything in it? Would He have any trouble finding them in His own world? But Adam and Eve were acting like children, thinking God could be fooled.

Before we blame those first two people and laugh at their scheme, we need to look at ourselves and admit the many times we, too, have tried to cover up our sinfulness, thinking we could fool God.

What children we are in our Christian actions! Let's be mature and face the truths that are found in God's holy Word.

ONE MORE THOUGHT: Our secret schemes and plans may be hidden from loved ones but never from God. Everything is known to Him.

27

His Flawless Ways

BIBLE READING: Genesis 1:26-31

Sometimes people consider themselves to be "creative," a word the dictionary says means "productive" or "imaginative."

As a young child I thought I would like to be a creator. The idea was there, but I had a little problem with the execution. Since my father was a carpenter, there were always pieces of lumber laying around the garage. I visualized a marvelous invention in my mind and then went to work measuring, sawing and nailing—everything I had seen my father do.

As some of the neighborhood children watched, they asked what I was doing. Boastfully I told them I was making a wagon. This intrigued them, so they stayed and watched as I put the pieces together, finishing by adding the wheels and handle.

Then came the big moment. Pulling my "creation" up a steep hill, I got in and away it went. Down, down, down. I had been successful. I had made a wagon. Almost!

As the wagon picked up speed, an awful problem became evident. There was no way to steer the wagon! I had put on a handle but no steering equipment.

I can still hear the laughter of my neighborhood friends. Moments before, they had been admiring me for my "talent." Now they were laughing. One thing was very clear. My creativity may have been characterized by thought, but the execution definitely lacked something!

But when God created the world, He had no problems either in thought or in execution. God made light, the sky, grass, trees, animals and man. And His work was flawless.

After He looked at the things He had made, He recognized that they were all good. Then God looked at His prize creation. He had made man in His own likeness, in His own image. When God looked at His man, He saw that this creation was not only good but that it was *very* good.

And God's goodness did not end with that day of creation. It continues today. Everything He does for us is good and perfect and cannot be improved upon in any way. At times we tend to feel that God does not understand our circumstances and that our ways may be better than His ways. But very soon we recognize that we are wrong and that God is perfectly right.

ONE MORE THOUGHT: As God's creation, we should willingly and joyfully follow His directions for us.

28

Inner or Outer Change?

BIBLE READING: Mark 10:17-22

American television commercials, newspaper and magazine ads often try to convince women that various lotions, creams and cosmetics can take away all the blemishes and wrinkles that age produces. But most doctors insist that outward applications are not the answer.

They tell us that most skin blemishes, wrinkles and other age marks come as a result of inner conditions. We are told that the best way to keep fit and look our best is to exercise properly, eat the right foods, drink plenty of water and get a full night's rest.

A young man came and knelt before Jesus one day and asked how he could inherit eternal life (John 10:17). Our Lord began by rehearsing some of the commandments that we now find in the Old Testament. To this the young man responded, "Why, I've kept all of those since I was just a young person" (see v. 20). And yet he went away sad because all of those outward observances were not enough to give this man eternal life.

To Nicodemus Jesus explained that a person has to be born again (see John 3). In other words, salvation from sin is an inner experience, not simply an outward change.

Some churches today encourage their congregations to remember the poor, the minorities and the less fortunate. "Do good works," they preach. "Share your money, love your neighbor, and when you do, you will enjoy eternal life."

But this is not true. While all of these actions are good, they are simply outward expressions and do not necessarily mean there has been an inner change of the sinful heart condition.

The only way anyone can really be changed is by coming to Christ and asking Him for complete forgiveness and newness of life. When this is done, then Jesus tells us, "Whosoever believeth in him should not perish, but have eternal life" (v. 15).

Treating your neighbor kindly, helping those in need and showing concern for those who are less fortunate are all good deeds. But doing good deeds was not enough for the rich young man, and it is not enough for us. We do not impress God by only doing good works. Showing Him and others that we are good people is like putting on face creams to try to take away the internally caused blemishes. The heart must be changed, and only God can make that change in your life.

Have you had this experience?

ONE MORE THOUGHT: Good deeds will never save you, but they are perfectly in order after God has changed your life.

29

That One Request

BIBLE READING: I Kings 3:5-14

If you have seen children when they are told to choose one gift from a large selection of toys, you know how hard it is for them to make a decision. They go from one item to another, trying to decide what they really want.

Every year my husband asks, "What would you like for your birthday?" or "What do you want for Christmas?" There are usually dozens of little items I could use for the house, but when I mention them, he says, "Those are house gifts. But what do *you* want?"

At that moment I can mention anything I want. (Of course, I know the budget limit, and I know what I can't ask for.) His wish is to get me something I would like.

Solomon was asked a similar question. From God's bountiful riches, Solomon could choose anything his heart desired. There was no limit. He did not have to think about price or budget. Think of the things he could have asked for! Everything in God's wonderful world was available to him at that moment. But Solomon chose wisely. He asked for the ability to discern between good and bad—wisdom to do what was right. And God was pleased with his request. As a result, the Lord showered not only wisdom upon Solomon but also gave him riches and honor and the promise of a long life if he would walk in God's ways.

If God were to ask us what we wanted more than anything else in the world, what would we choose? Would our thoughts and wishes be in line with what God would want to give us?

Material things have come to mean so much to people of our generation (Christians included) that our minds immediately go in that direction. Our selfish desires would probably lead us to ask for something that was beneficial only to us.

Be honest. What would you want if suddenly you were given the opportunity to make one request? Would it be money, education, travel, youth, health? All of these are things people talk about and say they would like. But would you choose one of these if you had only one choice?

Sometimes when we address God in public prayer meetings, we realize that others are also listening, so we suddenly put on a cover of spirituality and make this kind of request: "Give me more of Your love" or "Bless me with money to give to missions." We hope people will hear and will judge us accordingly. But these are not always honest petitions.

God's Word says, "Ask anything" (John 14:14). And if there is one need that most Christians should consider, it is for a heart that is fully tuned to God's will. Then when we pray, we know we will be asking for the very thing God wants to give us—an answer according to His perfect will.

ONE MORE THOUGHT: When God says, "Ask anything," He does not expect us to be selfish but to be grateful.

30

To Complain or to Thank?

BIBLE READING: Psalm 148

Isn't it easy to complain? The weather is too hot or too cold, there is too little rain or too much. We're not really sick, but we're not well either. Sure, there is an income in our home, but it's certainly not enough!

Complain, complain, complain. We all find ourselves trapped by this dreadful and sinful malady. We do agree, however, that other people complain too much and too often! When they do it, it is absolutely unnecessary. But when we do it, it is justified.

Ever since I had rheumatic fever (right after I graduated from Bible school), my sometimes-not-too-easy-to-move joints keep me from accomplishing certain feats. On a rainy morning, it becomes a chore to convince my legs that they must get themselves off the mattress and out of bed. Since all people do not have this problem, I should certainly have the right to complain, shouldn't I?

Then I look across the street, and there sits an 18-year-old boy. He has no joints to pain him, for he has no legs. Two weeks before he was to go to college on a football scholarship, a truck crushed his legs and both of them had to be amputated. Would he change places with me? Most certainly. Do I have anything to complain about? No. Thinking of him causes me to give thanks to the Lord for what I have.

A young mother complained loudly during a women's meeting about her lack of sleep. Because her little baby was having trouble adjusting to a new formula, he did not sleep well, and this caused her to be up much of the night. Next to her sat a guest who had lost her little one shortly after birth. Did the young mother complain anymore? No. After apologizing she went home and thanked the Lord that she still had her little boy, and she prayed for love and patience as he adjusted to the new food.

We take our sight for granted until we meet someone who is blind. We forget to be grateful for ears that hear until we meet a person who is deaf. Married women often fail to thank God for their husbands, homes and families until they realize there are many who are not blessed as they are.

Yes, it is very easy to complain until we examine the lives of others less fortunate. Then shamefully confessing our ungratefulness, we finally thank the Lord for what we have.

"O give thanks unto the Lord," the Bible says (Ps. 136:1). Let's use our time and breath to be grateful rather than to complain. He is honored so much more when we offer thanks than when we grumble and complain.

ONE MORE THOUGHT: God gave us tongues, breath and life to praise Him. Are we doing it?

31
It's Still There

BIBLE READING: Psalm 119:97-105

Missionaries often tell how God's Word directed them to a certain field of service. If they had depended on circumstances or feelings, they might have made a mistake. But trusting God's Word to lead them, they could not make an error.

As a student in Bible school I contracted diptheria. The disease left me with a serious heart condition. But I had dedicated myself to God for His service in whatever place He chose to use me. Now would my life be snatched away without an opportunity to serve Him? While praying about it, I asked the Lord to show me clearly what my future might be. He did through His Word. I had been reading the Psalms. That night in Chapter 118, verse 17, I read: "I shall not die, but live, and declare the works of the Lord."

Years later, I had to make another major decision—to marry or to remain single. I had spent many years serving the Lord through the ministry of Back to the Bible Broadcast. Now I had to know God's will in this matter. I prayed and read and read and prayed, fearful that I would make a mistake.

Before church one Sunday, I asked the Lord to use my pastor to help me make the right decision. His text that morning (Gen. 24:58) encouraged me to decide in favor of marriage.

Yes, God's Word has the answer to every question in life, but we so often neglect to seek it out. But it's still there.

ONE MORE THOUGHT: God's Word gives advice, answers, guidance and wonderful fellowship. Let's read it.